Francis Marion Crawford

Our Silver

A Letter Addressed to George S. Coe

Francis Marion Crawford

Our Silver
A Letter Addressed to George S. Coe

ISBN/EAN: 9783744766494

Printed in Europe, USA, Canada, Australia, Japan

Cover: Foto ©ninafisch / pixelio.de

More available books at **www.hansebooks.com**

A LETTER

ADDRESSED TO

GEORGE S. COE, Esq.,
Chairman of Executive Council of the American Bankers' Association.

BY

F. MARION CRAWFORD.

———◆———

NEW YORK:
Douglas Taylor, Printer, corner Fulton and Nassau Streets.

—

1881.

OUR SILVER.

I.

The chief point in which this country differs from others
in regard to the question of currency lies in the fact that,
whereas other countries are, generally speaking, under the
necessity of importing their currency in the first instance,
on the other hand America produces her own bullion; and
not only she produces a sufficient quantity to supply her
own present requirements, but also a large amount which
goes ultimately to supply the circulation of other countries. So great, however, is the productiveness of American mines that even after they have supplied the United
States and many other countries with the amounts required at home and abroad, it has hitherto been found
impracticable to force the circulation up to the figure which
represents the home coinage; or, in other words, to keep
the demand for coined dollars in any sort of equilibrium
with the supply. At the present time the excess of the
supply of silver dollars over the demand is roughly reckoned at $77,000,000, which are lying in the Treasury vaults
without any apparent prospect of coming into circulation,
but rather having an evident tendency to increase. The
question which now presents itself to financiers is: What
steps are necessary to restore the equilibrium between the
supply of silver produced by American mines and the
demand for silver in the United States and abroad? It
must be apparent to the most superficial observer what the
consequences must be if this question is not very shortly
answered, and if the remedy which must be supposed
embodied in that answer is not immediately applied. For,
if things continue in their present state, the supply exceed-
ing the demand, it is clear that the inactive surplus of

coined money will continue increasing, the value of silver will fall, and will only cease to fall when the point is reached at which a large number of mines will cease to be worked; in accordance with the well-known law, that the price of any product depends upon the cost of production where it is produced under the most disadvantageous circumstances, and its corollary, that no product will continue to be produced for any length of time under circumstances which do not admit of obtaining the ordinary rate of profit on the capital employed in production. The owners of all mines in which the cost of production exceeds a certain limit (and the number of such mines will soon become very great) will be obliged to stop work until, in the course of years, the surplus of inactive bullion has been sufficiently drawn off by wear and tear or other means to admit of those mines being again worked so as to afford at least the ordinary rate of profit on the capital employed. In practice, owing to speculation in stocks, mines frequently continue to be worked some time after they cease to be profitable.

It cannot be supposed that the owners of mines are ignorant of these laws, or of the prospect which awaits them, if things continue much longer in their present state —and in truth they have shown themselves active enough in supporting every scheme which has been brought forward with any show of reason as tending to keep up the value of the produce of their mines. Nevertheless, it appears that all remedies it has been attempted to apply are in themselves short-sighted; able, indeed, to maintain bullion values for a time, but utterly incapable of producing a permanent effect.

It is strange that, in the face of all that has been written on the subject by those great political economists who have reduced the treatment of commerce and finance to an exact science, the radical misconceptions in regard to the nature of money, which were pardonable enough a century ago, should still maintain so firm a hold on the public mind. The action of the United States in the Act of 1878, by which it was believed that the mining interests had been so greatly benefited, and the wild talk about bi-metallism, not to mention the longing of Western men for what might but too easily prove a return to inconvertible paper, are merely the expressions of a strongly rooted but diseased belief that money is not like anything else; that money does not conform to the laws of nature, but is mysteriously acted upon and directed in its channels by an inscrutable and demoniac agency. Until it is completely understood that money, and especially the precious metals for purposes of coinage, is a commodity precisely similar in its nature to the ordinary objects of trade, and that the use of it is nothing more than a mutual understanding among nations for purposes of obvious convenience, it must necessarily be out of the question to deal effectually with the phenomena which arise in natural consequence out of such a use of it. I am fully aware that in making these statements I am not saying anything original, nor is that my intention, persuaded as I am that the singular and somewhat alarming situation of the United States in regard to the silver question is as capable of immediate and permanent solution by the mere application of known laws as the simplest equation of two unknown quantities can be, the moment the value of the one is determined. In regard to money I will, before proceeding, quote at length a passage from J. S. Mill, embodying the best definition of what money is with which I am acquainted :

" Money, when its use has grown habitual, is the medium
" through which the incomes of the different members of the
" community are distributed to them, and the measure by
" which they estimate their possessions. As it is always
" by means of money that people provide for their different
" necessities, there grows up in their minds a powerful asso-
" ciation leading them to regard money as wealth in a more
" peculiar sense than any other article; and even those who
" pass their lives in the production of the most useful objects
" acquire the habit of regarding those objects as chiefly im-

" portant by their capacity of being exchanged for money.
" A person who parts with money to obtain commodities,
" unless he intends to sell them, appears to the imagination
" to be making a worse bargain than a person who parts
" with commodities to get money; the one seems to be
" spending his means, the other adding to them. Illusions
" which, though now in some measure dispelled, were long
" powerful enough to overmaster the mind of every poli-
" tician, both speculative and practical, in Europe.

" It must be evident, however, that the mere introduction
" of a particular mode of exchanging things for one another,
" by first exchanging a thing for money, and then ex-
" changing the money for something else, makes no differ-
" ence in the essential character of transactions. It is not
" with money that things are really purchased. Nobody's
" income (except that of the gold or silver miner) is derived
" from the precious metals. The pounds or shillings which
" a person receives weekly or yearly are not what consti-
" tutes his income; they are a sort of tickets or orders
" which he can present for payment at any shop he pleases,
" and which entitle him to receive a certain value of any
" commodity that he makes choice of. The farmer pays his
" laborers and his landlord in those tickets, as the most
" convenient plan for himself and them; but their real
" income is their share of his corn, cattle and hay, and it
" makes no essential difference whether he distributes it to
" them directly or sells it for them and gives them the price;
" but as they would have to sell it for money if he did not,
" and as he is a seller at any rate, it best suits the purposes
" of all that he should sell their share along with his own,
" and leave the laborers more leisure for work and the land-
" lord for being idle. The capitalists, except those who are
" producers of the precious metals, derive no part of their
" income from those metals, since they only get them by
" buying them with their own produce, while all other
" persons have their incomes paid to them by the capitalists,
" or by those who have received payment from the capi-

" talists, and as the capitalists have nothing from the first,
" except their produce, it is that and nothing else which
" supplies all incomes furnished by them. There cannot, in
" short, be intrinsically a more insignificant thing in the
" economy of society than money, except in the character
" of a contrivance for sparing time and labor. It is a
" machine for doing quickly and commodiously what would
" be done, though less quickly and commodiously, without
" it, and, like many other kinds of machinery, it only exerts
" a distinct and independent influence of its own when it
" gets out of order."—(J. S. MILL, Pr. of Pol. E., iii., 7, §3.)

It will be noticed in this definition that the case of mine
owners is mentioned as being the only one in which income
is derived from the precious metals, and it is of course con-
ceivable that, in this country, where the class of persons
who so derive their income is relatively very large, the
special case is sufficiently important to require special consideration in applying general laws. "There cannot," says
the definition, "be intrinsically a more insignificant thing,
" in the economy of society, than money, except in the
" character of a contrivance for sparing time and labor."
But though money is a machine to save labor like any other,
yet, in the case of all machines, the extent to which they are
used and the price paid for them is a question of vital
importance to those persons who make the machines. And
so with the American producer of money : it is as indispen-
sable for the maintenance of his income that the demand
for the money he produces should continue, as it is that
locomotives should continue to be used on railways, in
order that locomotive manufacturers may get the interest
of the capital they employ.

It has indeed been said that money has a twofold func-
tion : that it is a commodity, and also the medium of exchange. But its use as a medium is certainly limited. It
is as absurd to suppose it possible to increase the amount of
money required for exchange, unless the collective trade of

the world is extended, as it would be to try and force more
water through an inch pipe than it will carry, though the
reservoir supplying it were ever so large. After this fixed
necessity of trade has been supplied, then there is no
logical alternative possible for the strictest of economists
but to allow that all the money produced over and above
this is a simple commodity. And even if it is granted that
the character of money as a commodity is somewhat modi-
fied by circumstances attending its circulation, those circumstances do not exist in connection with money which
cannot circulate owing to its superfluity.

To those familiar with Mr. J. S. Mill's mode of reasoning,
the following is a more simple demonstration: Mr. Mill
proves at length that " the value of money depends on its
quantity combined with the rapidity of circulation." Obviously, when there is no circulation at all, the second factor
falls out, and the value of money which does not circulate
depends solely on the cost of its production. So that, even
by the strictest interpretation, the unemployed part, with
which we now have to do, conforms entirely to the definition of a commodity.

Superfluous money, then, is a commodity, and, therefore,
in countries which produce it in the shape of precious
metals, it is essential that there should be a market for it,
or it will not continue worth producing; and if it ceases to
be worth producing, those who own the land which yields
it are as badly off as a farmer would be if, by sudden isola-
tion or other cause, he were totally prevented from selling
any of the products of his land. And those who own
mines constitute in this country a class whose interests are
too considerable to be overlooked, and whose position is
sufficiently strong to give them an influential voice in the
government. These things are not in any sense matters of
opinion, but rather they are demonstrated facts, to question
which is merely to acknowledge a total ignorance of the
subject.

When it is admitted, as it must be, that silver in the

United States is a mere commodity, produced and brought to market by the mine owners in precisely the same way as grain is raised and sold by farmers, it may fairly be supposed that the same, or nearly similar, conditions apply to the one as to the other. We will suppose, as we have a right to do, that the phenomenon which now appears in the silver market had appeared instead in the cereal market. We suppose, then, that, in a given year, other things remaining the same, there has been a harvest of wheat of extraordinary abundance, the preceding years not having been attended by any scarcity. It is evident that, since there has been no scarcity, there has been enough in the country each year to supply the home market; in other words, that as much has been grown as could be consumed, or as the buyers in the country could in any case be induced to purchase for their own use. And the buyers of cereals in one shape or another are the entire population of the country without a single exception, for probably all Americans eat some kind of bread. The year under notice has by the hypothesis, however, produced a quantity more than usual—a quantity more than all the buyers in the country, that is, than all the population of the country, can possibly be induced to buy. It is clear that the growers of this extraordinary crop will not be satisfied to sell the same amount as usual for the usual rates, allowing the remainder to perish without bringing any increased profit. At first they will probably endeavor to increase the demand by lowering the price, hoping that at the cheaper rate the demand will be increased beyond the ratio of cheapness; as, for instance, that by lowering the price $\frac{1}{4}$, the public may be induced to take $\frac{1}{2}$ more, as constantly occurs in actual commerce. But by the hypothesis the population have not suffered from any scarcity, and will not consume any more cereals even at the reduced prices; on the contrary, if the growers, finding their attempt to force a demand fail, should again raise the price, it is probable that the consumers, being accustomed to the lower price, would for some time consume less than their average, preferring to deny themselves rather than pay the old figure. The sellers would, therefore, in no case be better off than if there had been no extraordinary harvest, and would very likely, if there were any difference, realize less profit on the home consumption than in any ordinary years. Obviously, if they wish to get a market for their surplus stores of cereals they must look elsewhere, namely, to foreign countries. They will carry their corn to market abroad.

It is highly probable that some other country produces some article which cannot be so cheaply produced at home, and of which home consumers would buy more if it were offered for sale. This article, then, will be at once selected by those who have surplus cereals to dispose of, as a suitable object of barter, and if the country which produces it will take the cereals to the extent to which they are offered the equilibrium will be restored, provided that the whole quantity of the newly imported article obtained in barter for the surplus cereals finds buyers in the home country. But if obstacles lie in the way of such a barter, so that, while the producer of cereals is unable to dispose of them at home, he cannot sell them or barter them abroad on such terms as to obtain some return, if ever so small, for his pains, he will abandon the attempt, and his best course will obviously be to hoard his surplus in the hope that he may be able to dispose of it at some future time. He does so, and just so much capital as is represented by his hoarded surplus will be lying inactive, that is, doing no good to himself or any one else. The example ends here. It is a complete case growing out of an hypothesis which it is perfectly reasonable to assume; and it is, moreover, a case which actually occurs in some parts of the United States, with the difference that the maize and wheat are consumed as fuel, and are thus of some small use, the obstacle to barter in such cases being the too great expense of transportation to the market. Though I have taken cereals as an example, because they are almost universally consumed in every civilized country, I clearly might have taken any other commodity in illustration, though the case would then have been less universally illustrative, owing to the restrictions attaching to commodities used more in one branch of society than another.

The example I have here imagined is only a particular instance in the general illustration of international demand and supply familiar to all political economists. Let us take the existing state of things in America in regard to the production of gold and silver, and see in what respects it coincides with the example I have described.

In America, as I have before said, silver and gold are commodities extracted from mines by means of labor paid for and capital laid out in the necessary tools and machinery by the capitalists who own the soil in which the mine lies. Mines, therefore, correspond to farms where the farmer owns the land, supplies the tools and employs labor. The produce of the mine, like the produce of the farm, must pay for the labor, maintain the owner, and yield besides at least as much profit as could be got for the employment of the same amount of capital elsewhere; otherwise the mine, like the farm, will cease to be worked. The miner, like the farmer, must convert his produce into money, which he does by selling it to the dealer. The dealer pays for the produce in money. So does the State or the exporter of bullion. The State deals in money and the exporter of bullion also deals in money, and here there arises a competition. The State has a strong interest in keeping specie in the country, and the exporter of bullion, as long as his trade is a profitable one (and when it is not so any longer he will cease to engage in it), has an equally strong interest in sending bullion out of the country. Now, in several countries, notably in those in which the metal it is desired to throw into circulation actually circulates, the State endeavors to attract bullion to the mint, by not only coining it *gratis*, but by returning to the producer a somewhat greater number of coins than his bullion is actually worth. It is true that this is effected by alloying the silver, but the State which issues these alloyed coins also engages to receive them in payment of debts to itself of a greater or less amount.

As long as the bullion exporter and the Government continue to make it worth the miner's trouble to produce the precious metals, just so long will he continue to do so, and no longer.

Before proceeding with the exposition of the situation it will be well to pause and eliminate all obviously unnecessary details from the case, as only tending to complicate it. In the first place we need practically deal only with one of the precious metals, since whatever is true of the one will be also true of the other. In America, the production and disposal of silver present very similar characteristics to those of gold, but many of them appear in a much higher degree of development, in proportion as the amount (not the value) of silver produced in the United States is far greater than the amount (not the value) of the gold, and still continues to increase, whereas gold has been produced at a nearly unvarying rate for the last twenty-five years; and consequently, conforms so far to all the conditions of any ordinary commodity, produced with the same regularity, that we may for the present postpone the consideration of it. We shall therefore deal solely with silver at present. Next, we may leave the exporter of bullion out of the question. For, as a matter of fact, his intervention is at present of small importance, the accumulations of silver being found in the hands of the Government, and not in those of the bullion exporter, whose operations are not nearly so extensive and are conducted on the principle of " small profits and quick returns." The case to be considered, therefore, as of the most general importance, is that in which the miner produces the silver and the State takes it for coinage, buying it of him and paying for it in currency. This has continued to occur to a considerable amount ever since it was supposed that the State must buy the silver and issue it to ensure its going into circulation ;

and it is principally this action which has caused the accumulation of considerable hoards of coined dollars in the vault of the treasury. As a matter of fact it did not require much foresight to see that this would be the very way to prevent its circulating, and that, if the Government had bought no silver but had contented itself with coining and returning to the owners what was brought to the mint, there would most probably have been, at the present moment, a larger number of silver dollars in circulation than there actually is of them; a fact which I shall presently show.

When in 1878 it was hastily decided to make silver circulate at any cost and large quantities of it were coined, it was determined to keep the dollar at a value which is made equal to 84½ cents, a fact which gave a great deal of trouble to certain moralists, who regarded it as a piece of Government dishonesty, and combined with their religious fervor a desire to export bullion. The necessity for keeping the dollar at a rate above its intrinsic value is, however, apparent at a glance. For if one dollar coin were worth exactly a dollar in value, a little change in the market value of silver would make it profitable to melt the coin and sell it for bullion; and this would be done every time the value of silver rose a little above what it was rated at when the currency was adjusted by law, and eventually a large part of the silver coinage would disappear in this way. It is therefore necessary to rate the dollar higher than its intrinsic value by as much as silver is likely to fluctuate, or in other words to coin the silver dollar so as to contain by weight a less number of cents actual value than 100. As the Government agrees to receive the silver dollar, as well as to pay it, there is obviously no dishonesty in the matter. The same thing is done in other countries, as in England for instance, and it is well known that the German gold coin of 20 marks contains about 20 pfennigs or 1 per cent. less gold than it is rated at. Of course, the fact of receiving back a greater number of dollars than the weight of the silver in bullion really represents, always acts as a great inducement to producers of silver to bring it to the mint to be coined, as they not only get their produce converted into coin for nothing, but also seem to receive something more than its value in addition.

Under these circumstances, if nothing else had been done, and if we suppose for the present that there were no trade with foreign countries, the producers of silver would go on bringing the metal to the mint and receiving back coined money for it; which they would pour into circulation, until the increase of money in circulation had so raised prices that the coin they offered would no longer buy so much of commodities as would compensate them for the trouble and expense of extracting silver from the mine and carrying it to the mint. At this point the production would be reduced, and in the course of time, by the slow process of wear and tear and similar causes, the amount of the circulation would be diminished so much as to lower prices and make it again profitable to work the mines. By this process there would probably be no hoarding of silver of any importance; and even if there were, the hoarded coin would remain in the hands of the producers. Of course, the keeping back of bullion could not occur until it resulted from the high prices of other commodities. But the Government did not perceive that by this means as much silver would inevitably be forced into circulation as people could possibly make use of. They supposed that for some occult reason miners would not bring their silver to the mint, and they determined to buy bullion, coin it, and send it into circulation, giving their creditors the option of receiving their dues in gold or silver.

Now, it is clear that the miner who presents bullion at the mint would be very willing to get back for his pains a greater number of dollars than his bullion represents in gold, and is always willing to sell it to the State while the State pays better for it than the bullion dealer. But the public will be strongly and reasonably prejudiced against accepting in payment a number of dollars, the intrinsic value of which is less than the value of what is due to them, reckoned in gold; and the public will insist to the uttermost on being paid in the more valuable coinage, or in convertible paper which can be at any time exchanged for gold. Hence it is that, whereas the dollars which miners would get for their silver would be put into circulation by themselves, yet the dollars which the Government coins from bullion it has purchased can never be disposed of to anything like the full amount of the coinage ; a great part of such coinage remaining hoarded in the Treasury vaults because no one can be found to take it.

The parallel between the case of silver as it is, and the imaginary case of cereals as I described it, is now complete. By a series of circumstances the supply of silver has now become greater than the demand for it ; for, if there were a demand, Government would not be obliged to store away its dollars instead of using them. It is true that the country might be induced to absorb a little more by the miners themselves, who, however, must part with their silver at a diminution of price, equivalent to what is called the depreciation of silver. But as far as the Government is concerned, there is as much silver circulating as the public can possibly be induced to take on the present terms. And we have seen that the public is not unreasonable in refusing to take dollars as such, which contain only 84½ cents worth of silver, so long as they can obtain gold, or notes convertible into gold, instead. Under these circumstances, in a country not producing its own silver, but importing it, the importation would diminish at once, as it would in the case of any other article of commerce. But America produces her own silver, and like the rest of her productions she must have a permanent market for it, or a portion of her capital will be idle, and her active wealth will be reduced.

As for the sake of clearness I have hitherto omitted the consideration of foreign trade, so, now that I have shown how the accumulation of silver has taken place, I may introduce the element of commerce with foreign nations. For, obviously, when it is found that the country will not take any more silver for its own use, the only logically possible alternatives are that the surplus silver should not be used at all, or should be used outside of the country. But it is also certain that as long as a possibility of using the silver outside of the country exists, those who possess it will not be content with not using it at all; therefore, if there were no obstacles in the way, all the surplus silver, not required for actual circulation, for reserve funds, and for purposes of art and decoration in the United States, would find its way to foreign countries. If this had occurred, of course silver would not have lost value, as it would not have become a "drug" in the market. But it has not occurred yet, and we turn to the examination of the obstacles which must necessarily exist in the way of it.

II.

When a country has a surplus of some commodity which she desires to dispose of she can only dispose of it by taking in exchange some other commodities which she can make use of. And this means that the commodities which she receives in exchange must be such as will be sold after they have been imported. This, again, can only take place if, after having imported them, all expenses being paid, the articles can be sold in the country for as much more than was represented by the value of the exported article, while still on the spot, as is equivalent to the ordinary rate of profit on the capital embarked. Insurance, tariff duties, the part of the cost of carriage ultimately borne by the importing country, and other minor items are counted as part of the expenses to be written off before the profit on the capital is reckoned. If these expenses become too great the importer will either not make the profit which is necessary in order that he may continue trading, which will happen if he does not raise his prices; or, if he raises his prices, the public will not buy all of the commodity he imports, and he will be forced to contract his operations. In either case a diminution of trade to the point at which it remains profitable must be the natural and rapid result of obstacles put in the way of it.

These obstacles may be of two kinds. They may be inherent in the commodity itself or they may be due to wholly independent causes, which do not directly affect the commodity itself, but raise the price of the articles obtained in exchange for it. To the first class belong fluctuations in the amount or quality of the commodity, which tend to diminish its own value in the foreign markets without affecting other articles of commerce. As, for instance, if we suppose a sudden and great increase in the production of cereals, so that more is offered for sale all over the world than can possibly be bought, whereby the value of them is so much diminished that a sufficient quantity of commodities can no longer be obtained for a given quantity of cereals to make it profitable to transport cereals to market. To the second class belongs everything which tends to increase the price (not the original value) of the articles obtained in exchange for the commodity in such a manner as to diminish the existing demand for those articles in the country which takes them, by putting them out of the reach of a number of persons who were willing to take them at the lower price, but prefer to forego them at the higher price. For instance, when the surplus of a commodity is exported and articles are obtained in exchange for it which can be sold so as to make the trade profitable to those who engage in it; if the Government of the country imposes a tariff duty on those articles, it is clear that, if the law is not dishonestly evaded, the price of those articles in the country which has the tariff will rise exactly by the amount of tariff, other things remaining the same. It is probable that this rise of price will be such as to reduce permanently the demand for those articles unless those who engage in the trade be content with a much smaller profit on their capital; and if they are not content they must contract their operations.

These are the two classes of obstacles which are likely to arise.

Applying what has been deduced to the case of the production of silver in the United States, it becomes clear at once that the exportation of superfluous silver (and I repeat that it must be superfluous or it would not be lying idle) is checked by one or both of two obstacles; either by fluctuations in the value of silver itself, so that it will not buy enough saleable commodities to make it worth exporting, or by a tariff duty on the commodities which might be imported, so high as to diminish the demand for them too far to make it profitable to import more of them than are at present imported; or by both these causes acting simultaneously. And the extent to which the exportation of the superfluous yield of silver is checked is exactly equal to the amount at any time lying idle in the country, over and above the reserve fund necessary to maintain a convertible paper circulation, usually estimated at one-third of that circulation, and over and above the amount of metal used for purposes of art and luxury.

Now that we have arrived at these plain conclusions, it requires little but the most ordinary common sense to see that, supposing both the causes above stated to be at work in checking the availability of silver for commercial purposes in the United States, no remedy can be permanently effected which does not deal radically with both those causes. As a matter of fact they both really exist, for the value of silver is in a constant state of fluctuation, and at the same time heavy tariffs place a number of commodities, which would be eagerly bought if cheaper, entirely beyond the reach of the great majority of incomes in this country. The remedies applied must, therefore, be twofold and distinct; the one lying in persuading the rest of the world to do something which shall establish the value of silver at a standard less changeable than has hitherto been found practicable; the other consisting in a modification of the tariff duties to suit the altered conditions of the country.

Those remedies are, then :

A universal gold and silver standard.

A revision of the tariff.

Before proceeding, I wish to disclaim any belief in the magical properties of the words "Double Standard," or "Free Trade." The latter, in its true acceptation, defines an ideal state of commerce, in which every commodity would be produced in the place where it could be produced most advantageously; but which implies also an ideal state of society in which war should be impossible, and an ideal state of natural science in which any kind of scarcity would be foreseen and prevented. The expression "Double Standard" really implies the power to regulate absolutely the value of the precious metals all over the world. But though both these conditions are impossible, it is not out of the question to approach indefinitely near to either of them. In not believing in perfect free trade as a possibility, one is not expected to believe the existing system of tariffs to be perfection; and though far from asserting that a double standard will enable Russia and Austria to return to specie payments, one may be pardoned for anticipating a greater stability of silver from the combined action of a dozen rich governments, making it legal tender.

The late Mr. J. Stuart Mill disposed of the question of double standard in exactly three pages, showing it to be " a fond thing vainly imagined." The ground he took was that, as the values of the metals gold and silver in relation to each other are liable to fluctuate, the one would generally be worth more than the other. By " Gresham's law," that the inferior medium of circulation always drives out the more valuable when the circulation becomes redundant, a nation with a double standard would, he argued, alternately have a gold or a silver standard according as the one were more valuable than the other. All that would be got would be an increased item of expenditure for recoining every time the values altered. But in many places Mr. Mill was accustomed to say that it was impossible to foresee what position might arise, as no one could know how far the production of silver and gold would continue. It seems probable, therefore, that he might have been led, had he lived, to change his mind in regard to the double standard. He would have seen, as we see to-day, that though the relative fluctuation of the precious metals is the strong objection to a double standard, nevertheless, in the absence of a double standard, there is no means left by which to control that fluctuation at all. And if it is desirable to control the fluctuations of ordinary articles in the market, how much more should every one wish to steady the value of silver; which, double standard or no double standard, is, nevertheless, common money all the world over. Fortunately, there is a sufficient feeling in the United States at present in favor of a double standard to make it possible for me to pass over the details of its working and go on to the other step which must be taken to reduce the equation of international demand. That other step, as I before said, is the modification of the tariff.

The introduction of a double standard all over the world, though it would act as a fly-wheel to partially regulate the value of silver, would not in any extensive way tend to draw off the superfluous silver of the United States. It is quite true that at the first introduction of the double standard abroad, considerable quantities of silver bullion would be required to supply the new coins which would be needed. But when once this first outlay, so to speak, had been made, there would be no more bullion required than before, except to supply the wear and tear of foreign currencies. If, then, after the first movement, America went on producing silver at the same rate as at present, a return to the present state of affairs would be inevitable; and there would not even be the prospect of such temporary relief as has been obtained in the first case by the demand for bullion abroad on the extension of the currency. The advantage of the double standard, as far as it would affect the surplus production of American silver, would be a purely temporary one. In its relation to commerce, by establishing the market value of silver on a firmer basis, the advantage would be permanent. The only plan by which the surplus wealth of the country could be employed as capital would be by enlarging the country's financial operations. To accomplish this a permanent demand must be created for commodities (over and above what are at present sold in the country), which on the whole shall exchange for the regular annual surplus production of silver in the United States. The only way to do this is to raise the sluice which holds foreign imports out of the country, and let enough flow in to establish equilibrium. The tariffs must be lightened somewhere. I am aware of the extreme delicacy of this point, well understanding the vastness of the manufacturing interests at stake. Any attempt to diminish import duties at short notice must be attended with great danger, unless carried out according to a fixed and faultless scheme. But here is no question of any sweeping measure for introducing free trade. We only need a sufficient, though homœopathic, dose of free trade to enable us to enlarge our operations. But if the country is willing to say: "No! we will allow our capital to lie in vaults bearing no profit to ourselves, in order that our great-grandchildren may drink imitation hock and champagne grown on American soil," then I have nothing more to say. Such magnificent self-denial is becoming to the sons of free men. If this country prefers to use bad articles itself, and pay high prices for them, or not to get them at all, in order that its posterity may be clothed in purple and fine linen, and smoke Turkish tobacco of Virginia growth, the case is altered. Probably it would be

nearer the truth to credit the people with more financial
acumen and less thirst for domestic glory. In this case
they, like other business men, will be anxious to keep the
whole of their capital in active employment. But these
are mere statements. My business is with facts and their
logical consequences. I do not wish to appeal to the senti-
ment of politicians of my own country, but to the common
sense of honest men. A slight extension of the reasoning
I have already used will suffice.

Let us suppose it has been determined to revise the
tariff to a sufficient extent to admit of the surplus silver of
the United States being disposed of in exchange for commodities. A commission will be at once appointed to en-
quire into the alterations of the tariff which are possible.
Its duty will be to point out what articles, of a nature likely
to find a sale, can be imported in the greatest quantities
without prejudice to American manufacture. Doubtless
this task will not be a very easy one, though if the whole
commerce of the United States be compared with the value
of the additional capital it is sought to invest, it will be seen
that the extension is not so great as would at first be
imagined. It is probably not so great as to involve the
discontinuance of any branch of manufacture now success-
fully conducted. To enlarge the trade of such a country as
ours by an amount which does not exceed, or even equal,
the private fortunes of several of our richest men, is surely
not an undertaking to dishearten financiers. And what is
necessary does not mean more than this. And it must be
remembered that this extension does not amount to a
greater annual extension (after the first measures), than the
annual surplus of the silver production. The number of
millions, whatever it may really be, now lying idle, it has
taken some years to accumulate, whereas if that money had
been thrown into trade *pari passu* with its production, no
such accumulation would have occurred. Nor if the obstacles to an extension of trade were sufficiently removed,

could it occur again. The throwing, say, of 100 millions of dollars into the circulation of the world would not be felt much; perhaps it would not even raise prices generally all over the world; though the same increase made in the circulation of coin inside of the United States, if it were possible, would raise prices in the United States in a short time in exactly the ratio which 100 millions bears to the circulation of the whole country. Consequently, if we can throw 100 millions into the circulation* of the world without raising prices much anywhere, we obtain the whole of the advantage arising from the possession of 100 millions more money than our neighbors, with the same purchasing power. The only problem is to apply this purchasing power to the acquisition of commodities which we want, but cannot at present produce in sufficient quantities or of sufficiently good quality to satisfy those of us who either are, or would like to be, consumers of them. The commission appointed ought to have no great difficulty in pointing out what those articles are; and as a full satisfaction of the desire for all foreign articles which now exists in the United States, would, without doubt, require a much larger investment of capital than the surplus silver production now places at our disposal, it would, from the nature of things, be easy to make use of just so much of our reserve power of extension as should produce a permanent equilibrium. An examination of the existing tariff would require more space and technical discussion than is warranted in a pamphlet of the present dimensions; it is sufficient to point out that the importation of such things as foreign wines, silks and cloths, not to mention works of art and taste, and books, is capable of very great extension ; and that the lightening of the duties on such as these could

---

* Putting the circulation of the world at, say ten thousand millions, the proportion for prices would be $10,000,000,000 : 10,100,000,000 : : y : 101\text{-}100\ y$, which represents a theoretical possibility of a rise of one per cent. at the outside.

not but act as a stimulus to American industry. For American manufacturers would not long be content to be outdone by any others.

It seems to me that before leaving the subject it will not be out of place to examine briefly in what way a considerable modification of the tariff may be expected to affect securities and the stock market. If a sum of money is thrown into trade and it is properly managed, it is clear that, supposing there are a million more dollars sent out of the country, there ought to be a million dollars worth more of commodities coming into the country, and as the capital already seeking investment in securities forms no part of the million dollars taken from the hoarded surplus, so the investment of such capital will not of itself be affected in any way whatsoever. And so in any case where the extension of trade does not go beyond what is actually lying idle as surplus. And a very ordinary amount of foresight will be sufficient to prevent this. If the measures are not well considered, so that by the injury done to the manufacturers of certain articles any considerable amount of capital is suddenly liberated by the closing of works, it may be foretold that the price of securities will rise to an inflated condition to be followed by a crisis. But such a circumstance, as it constitutes a known danger, can also be securely guarded against. If, on the other hand, by lightening the tariff too much, a great inducement is offered to engage in foreign trade, too much capital will go out of the country, and the price of securities will fall. This too sudden lightening of duties is even easier to avoid by due caution than it will be to guard against errors in the selection of commodities on which the duties shall be lightened, in which latter case a greater multiplicity of interests will be called into play. But neither of the two presents any very great difficulty, provided the commission is composed of disinterested men of sound judgment and a fair knowledge of the subject.

That some time would be required in order to make the

necessary inquiries and arrangements, and that a law affecting the tariff ought never to be introduced without giving considerable notice, are points which must be considered, but which cannot be raised in objection. It is much to be regretted that the Conference which has been sitting in Paris should not yet have been successful in bringing about an immediate adoption of the double standard by at least one of the other countries there represented. If even one country could be induced to join us, an immediate easing of the silver market would ensue, which, though of course only a temporary relief, as I have already pointed out, would give us time for the consideration and study of the permanent remedy.

If, however, as first supposed, both mistakes are carefully avoided, the price of securities can only be affected indirectly by the improvement in trade, causing a more rapid increase of capital. Prices may, indeed, in such a case rise, but unless from independent circumstances, with which we have nothing to do, they will not become inflated and the improvement will be permanent.

A word must be said about the so-called "soft money" movement. I cannot see what difficulties this question presents which cannot be immediately explained. At all events, if the position of the soft money advocates is not clear we must allow at once that the valuable studies of American currency embodied in the books of Professors Francis A. Walker and William G. Sumner are utterly worthless, which the most hardened skeptic will hardly be prepared to state. Now it is an established law that a convertible paper currency is a direct gain to the issuers, and that as long as it remains strictly convertible it is not a loss to any one. The necessary condition attached to a convertible paper currency is that specie must be held in reserve to the extent of one-third of the whole paper circulation. By this means the paper will always circulate at par, and the whole amount of the precious metals thus freed from the duty of performing the part of money becomes available as a strict commodity, if so desired. Now the United States Government has unintentionally gravitated into this position. Its paper currency, being good for gold and circulating everywhere at par, is preferred on account of its convenience, which explains the constant demand for more of it. The reluctance on the part of the Government to accede to this demand is due to a just appreciation of the dangers threatening the country the moment the *amount* of paper in circulation becomes great enough to create a doubt in the public mind in regard to the immediate convertibility of the notes into gold. Need anything more be said? The limit to which paper may be issued is known, for it must be regulated so that the reserve fund of specie shall always be equal to one-third of the actual circulation. The question is answered.

To sum up: The position of affairs shows a country possessed of more silver than will circulate. The redundance of silver, together with certain circumstances connected with the currencies of foreign countries, causes at the same time a continual and considerable fluctuation in its value.

To secure greater stability in the value of silver, and to introduce measures for the permanent disposal of the surplus production of silver, are the necessary conditions for restoring the equilibrium destroyed by instability of value and redundance of amount.

The means for obtaining these conditions are the adoption of a double standard by as many countries as can be persuaded to do so, and a suitable revision of the tariff. The full accomplishment of both these conditions is necessary to the perfect restoration of equilibrium, but either measure separately will produce a partial restoration.

If, on the one hand, the introduction of the double standard in foreign countries should prove a task too heavy for the strength of our political influence abroad; yet, on the other hand, the reformation of our tariff is an operation entirely in our power, and which should have been undertaken in any case, whether we had been driven to it by force of circumstances or not. We have been driven to it.

The state of our tariff compared with the state of our productive power, or, to use the expression current in this country, of our potentiality, is an anachronism—a thing of the past. There were causes which were thought to justify its introduction, but they have disappeared, and it is high time that a beginning be made towards reforming the laws affecting our foreign commerce. We have advantages of position, of natural and developed resources, such as no other country in the history of the world has ever possessed before, or by the utmost stretch of what seems possible can ever possess again. We have also the advantage of all the accumulated experience and wisdom of mankind to guide us, merely requiring us to apply to each new position those laws which, resting on relentless logic and absolute truth, will neither suffer contradiction nor lead us into error. If, while wielding the gigantic powers of knowledge and wealth, we submit to having our actions influenced and our lives guided by petty considerations of personal vanity unworthy of the age we live in, our Nation will surely be one day called upon to render an account of her misdoings at the tribunal of mankind. And mankind will not be lenient.

F. MARION CRAWFORD.

NEWPORT, August 1st, 1881.

www.ingramcontent.com/pod-product-compliance
Lightning Source LLC
Chambersburg PA
CBHW021459090426
42739CB00009B/1795